Why DOGS Do That

Why DOGS Do That

Text by Tom Davis
Illustrations by Peter Ring

WILLOW CREEK PRESS

Minocqua, Wisconsin

Published by Willow Creek Press
P.O. Box 147
Minocqua, Wisconsin 54548

Designed by Heather M. McElwain

Library of Congress Cataloging-in-Publication Data
Davis, Tom.
    Why dogs do that : a collection of curious canine
behaviors / text by Tom Davis ; illustrations by Peter
Ring.
          p.   cm.
    ISBN 1-57223-139-4
    1. Dogs--Behavior--Miscellanea.   I. Title.
SF433.D38   1998   98-30019
636.7--dc21   CIP

Printed in Canada

TABLE OF CONTENTS

PREFACE

For as long as there have been dogs—15,000 years, give or take a few millennia—humans have been trying to figure out why they do the things they do. This is faintly ironic, given the fact that the dog is, in a very real sense, our handiwork, the product of our incessant tinkering with the machinery of nature. The thing that makes dogs so fascinating, and yet so perplexing, is that at times they seem almost human—and at other times they seem utterly alien. Author Edith Wharton referred to this dichotomy as the "us-ness" and "not-usness" with which every dog is endowed. We have made the dog in our own image, and we see reflected there the qualities that we'd like to think we possess: loyalty, courage, perseverance, compassion, selflessness, generosity, an astonishing capacity to love. As James Thurber, who understood dogs as well as anyone, put it, "If I have any beliefs about immortality, it is that certain dogs I have known will go to heaven, and very, very, few persons."

Trouble is, beneath its human veneer a dog is still a dog, with the same basic needs, urges, and instincts as the wolves from which it is descended (and with which, genetically speaking, it remains virtually identical). This is why we find so many aspects of canine behavior puzzling—and occasionally appalling. For example, the average person who considers his or her dog a member of the family is hard-pressed to reconcile its obvious relish for carrion, excrement, etc. The sexual indiscriminateness of most dogs also tends to give pet owners pause.

The problem, or course, is that we fall into the trap of applying human values to canine behavior. We "anthropomorphize," to use a word much bandied about these days. Viewed from a clear-eyed evolutionary perspective, however, most of the things dogs do make perfect sense. In the wild, where survival is the bottom line, any behavior that furthered the cause was eventually incorporated at the genetic level. It became instinctive, in other words, and while humans have selectively refined, augmented, and/or toned down these instincts to suit their own purposes, there is a cluster of core behaviors that all dogs, no matter how dissimilar they appear or how unrelated their intended function, have in common. A pointer may point, a retriever may retrieve, a sled dog may pull, and a hound may follow a scent trail in full cry. At heart, though, they're all a lot more alike than they are different.

Why Dogs Do That is a humble attempt at fitting together some of the pieces of the canine puzzle. The book is meant to be both enlightening and entertaining, meaning that the reader is required to exercise a certain amount of old-fashioned common sense in separating the factual (or what is at least the prevailing opinion) form the tongue-in-cheek. Sticklers for scientific exactitude will no doubt find many of the explanations wanting. Well, so be it. This book is for the general interest reader and dog lover, not the specialist, and anyone who cites it to support his or her academic agenda is definitely barking up the wrong tree. The hope is that the reader will come away with a better understanding of what makes dogs tick, a deeper appreciation of the qualities that endear them to us, and, most important of all, a renewed commitment to according them the care, respect, and devotion they so richly deserve.

Laughter is encouraged, too.

1.

WHY DO MALE DOGS LIFT THEIR LEGS?

Well, for one thing, if they stood on all fours, the way pups do (and the way adult dogs will sometimes do in situations of pressing urgency), they'd run the risk of splashing themselves on the backs of their forelegs. This is definitely uncool—sort of the canine equivalent of what happens to certain men when they're not paying attention to business, and as they go to zip up discover that they've rained on their trousers. More to the point, though, when a male dog lifts his leg he's in essence leaving his calling card.

While there may be an element of territoriality involved—"This is my turf, man"—it's primarily a social gesture, a way of announcing to other dogs "I was here." In canine society as in human, it's important to stay in circulation, frequent the trendiest fire hydrants, etc. And, reminiscent of the contests in which young boys so gleefully engage, there's a bit of one-upmanship (updog-ship?) in the way every leg-lifter tries to make his mark just a tad higher than the last passerby. This can result in some truly awesome displays of balance, flexibility, and marksmanship.

2.

WHY DO MALE DOGS LIFT THEIR LEGS ON YOUR FAVORITE SHRUBS?

This is one of those irksome behaviors that can variously be attributed to a perverse streak in the canine personality, a wicked sense of humor, and/or the rearing of jealousy's ugly head. It's almost as if the dog's saying, "If you're gonna shower all that attention on a rosebush, I'm damn well gonna *shower* the rosebush."

Of course, given the fact that dogs don't necessarily view urinating on something as a form of passing judgment (although I'm convinced that it can be; how else to explain those instances in which a dog very calmly and deliberately lifts its leg on a deserving person?), it could just be their way of participating in one of your favorite hobbies. Dogs, like kids, hate feeling left out. And it just might have something to do, too, with the aromas emitted by the assorted fertilizers and emulsions that gardeners so lovingly lavish on their prize plants.

3.

WHY DO FEMALE DOGS SQUAT?

Actually, not all of them do— or at least not all of them do all of the time. Quite a few females, particularly those with dominant personality traits, lift their legs as boldly and assertively as their male counterparts. And females in season will lift their leg to help "advertise" their availability.

It must be admitted, however, that they rarely attain the lofty heights (nor exhibit the triumphant arcs) of which the male is capable. It's a simple matter of anatomy, the same reason boys write their names in the snow and girls don't. Canine or human, there's no getting around the fact that the male is better-equipped for directional urination—a dubious claim to fame, perhaps, but hey, we'll take it.

4.

WHY DO DOGS DIG HOLES?

To fully understand canine behavior, you have to remember that if you scratch a dog, you find, beneath the surface, a wolf. Advances in DNA analysis have proved that the dog is not only descended from the wolf, but is in fact a wolf subspecies—hence the revision of the dog's taxonomic classification from *Canis familiaris* to *Canis lupus* familiaris (the wolf is *Canis lupus*). Over the millions of years of the wolf's existence, digging—to excavate dens, extract hidden prey, or simply create a cool place to lie down—became an instinctive behavior, a survival skill hard-wired into the genetic circuitry. In other words, dogs, which have been around for a mere 15,000 years or so, dig—whether we want them to or not. It's often a symptom of boredom, something like the sundry destructive behaviors exhibited by kids when the little angels have "nothing better to do."

As a footnote, the digging ability of terriers, breeds developed in the British Isles specifically to hunt "ground game" such as badgers, foxes, otters, etc., was one of the qualities for which they were originally prized, qualities that caused them to be known in antiquity as "earth dogges." A contemporary home owner surveying the cratered ruins of his or her backyard is likely to call them by other, more colorful, names.

5.

WHY DO DOGS BURY BONES?

Essentially, dogs bury bones for the same reason squirrels bury nuts: as a hedge against the lean times. Not that the typical dog has to worry about where his next meal will come from, but his wild ancestors figured out a long time ago that when food is easy to come by, it's a good idea to put some aside—kind of like setting up a savings account that can be drawn on in an emergency. This behavior is called "caching," and it's common among wolves and certain species of foxes as well as dogs. (When I find it necessary to feed my dogs in their travel crates during hunting trips, my English setter female will "cache" any leftovers by very carefully covering her bowl with a layer of straw.)

My impression, though, judging by the prevalence of the theme in the popular art, literature, and film (including cartoons) of the early and mid-20th century, is that dogs aren't burying bones the way they used to. Not that they're any less interested; the more likely explanation is that they're simply not getting the opportunity, the veterinary profession having done a pretty thorough job educating dog owners about the consequences of a shard of bone lodging in their pet's digestive tract. The jaws of the average dog, after all, can generate several hundred pounds per square inch of crushing force, more than enough to splinter even the toughest beef bone.

6.

WHY DO DOGS BARK INCESSANTLY WHEN TIED UP OR CLOSELY CONFINED?

Dogs bark for a variety of reasons: to express fear, aggression, or excitement, to sound a warning, to invite other dogs to play, the list goes on. In the case of the dog that's tied up or confined to a small area, barking is often a symptom of boredom and/or general discontentment. Frankly, many dogs that are kept in such conditions have been poorly socialized, and receive very little attention, affection, and "quality time" that make dogs well-adjusted citizens. Also, as the dog's "territory" shrinks, it feels exposed and insecure, growing increasingly sensitive to the perception of threat (also see #23).

Years ago, an insurance company terminated my home owner's policy because one of my setters barked unceasingly at the inspector they'd dispatched to look things over. I was living in the country at the time, and my dogs were staked to chains that allowed them to comfortably enter their wooden houses but restricted their movements to a circumscribed radius. Unannounced, the insurance man, a total stranger, was not warmly greeted by old Zack (who didn't have a mean bone in his body). He probably wouldn't have been so vociferous if he'd had the luxury of a fenced run. (For the record, an insurance company with a keener understanding of canine psychology was happy to provide me with coverage.)

7.

WHY DO DOGS MOUNT YOUR GUEST'S LEG?

This behavior, which is most often seen in younger dogs (although some friends of mine had a middle-aged Bassett that was incorrigible in this respect), is nature's way of preparing them for the Real Thing. Practice makes perfect, in other words. Some females—again, generally younger ones—will hump your leg, too, almost as if they're trying to sort out their sexual identity. A few never do; or should I say, in this era of political correctness, that they "choose an alternative lifestyle," homosexual behavior among dogs being more common than you might suspect.

8.

WHY DO DOGS CHASE CARS?

All dogs, to one degree or another, chase. It's instinctive, a manifestation of the "prey drive" without which their wild forebears could not have survived. Something moves, and the wolf—or the untrained dog—chases it. This genetically programmed response to motion is what makes a weasel, for example, kill every chicken in the henhouse. It's not that the weasel's "blood-thirsty"; rather, it's simply reacting in the way it has evolved to react.

Some canine behaviorists have gone so far as to suggest that dogs chase cars because they "mistake" them for the large wild ungulates, such as moose, that constitute such a significant percentage of the wolf's prey base. It's certainly true that a moose is as big as a lot of cars, and, drawing another parallel, it's equally true that moose wound, maim, and even kill their fair share of wolves. The flip side of this coin is that some wolf-moose encounters end successfully, at least from the wolf's perspective. The same cannot be said of the typical dog-car encounter, to which the only happy ending is a dog that escapes injury and—you hope—learns a lesson it will never forget.

9.

WHY DO DOGS CHASE THEIR TAILS?

Because they're there, of course. Watch a dog as it chases its tail, and you can almost hear it thinking, "What is this thing that keeps following me around, and why can't I catch it?" Quantifying canine intelligence is a very tricky business; there are dogs that display great aptitude for obedience work yet don't have the sense to come in out of the rain, and dogs that are seemingly untrainable yet exhibit astonishing reasoning and decision-making powers.

It's a pretty safe bet, though, that a dog that persists in chasing its tail wasn't at the front of the line when the brains were being distributed—although, in fairness to the dog, prolonged and repeated tail chasing can also be symptomatic of seizures brought on by a serious epileptic-type disorder. If your pet exhibits such behavior, get it to a veterinarian, pronto.

10.

WHY DO DOGS ROLL IN VILE THINGS LIKE DECAYING CARP?

There are a couple of theories, by no means mutually exclusive, that explain why dogs take such obvious and unabashed delight in rolling in stuff that makes us gag: excrement, carrion (the older and fouler, the better), anything and everything that is rotten, putrid, and deliquescent. And they don't just roll in it; wriggling joyfully on their backs, they do their damnedest to smear it around and rub it in. The more specific hypothesis suggests that dogs roll in stinky stuff to mask their own scent, and thus gain an edge over prey species (remember: scratch a dog, find a wolf) that might otherwise detect them and flee. (Contemporary human deer hunters do much the same thing when dousing their clothing with various bottled scents.)

The other theory, more general in application, holds that it's a way for a dog to tell other dogs where they've been and what they found there. A dog streaked with excrescence is viewed by his brethren as a storyteller, and canine society holds story-tellers in high esteem. This much is certain: Old-time hound handlers and bird dog trainers agree that the dogs with the best noses are the ones most inclined to cover themselves in excrement. Given the fact that an average dog has some 220 million scent receptors (a human has a paltry 5 million), it really makes you wonder.

11.

WHY DO DOGS EAT VILE THINGS LIKE HORSE APPLES AND COW PIES?

Animals in general are not plagued by the Fear of Excrement that haunts humankind. Many winter birds—wild turkeys, for example—depend on the "hot lunch program": cow manure which they pick through for kernels of undigested grain and other tasty nuggets. Other species practice "self-recycling," routinely ingesting their own scat. Rabbits literally must consume their own feces to obtain certain vitamins critical to their survival. Dogs eat horse apples, cow pies, and the like because their wild ancestors, rather than dying of starvation when normal fare couldn't be found, adapted to eating anything that had nutritive value, including excreta. In this regard, think of wolves—and, therefore, dogs—as carnivores by nature, but omnivores by necessity.

Of course, there's probably nothing more repulsive than the sight of an adored pet—the same animal that frenziedly licks your face, given the chance—gobbling its own stools, or those of its kennelmates. (The technical term for this behavior, by the way, is "coprophagy.") Dogs are great imitators, and it's believed that one of the reasons they do this is to imitate what they observe you doing when you pick up after them. And because dogs pick things up with their mouths, the rest comes more or less naturally. Ironically, the tremendous improvements in the quality of dog food over the past decade or so have, in all likelihood, made this behavior even more common.

12.

WHY DO DOGS LICK THEMSELVES, AND OTHER DOGS?

Among other reasons, dogs lick to cleanse themselves, facilitate the healing of wounds, and soothe skin irritations. Licking can also be an expression of boredom or nervousness, the result of which is often a knobby sore on the carpal joint (the dog's "wrist") called a "lick granuloma."

Dams lick their puppies to clean them (thus removing scent that could be detected by predators) and stimulate breathing and elimination. Males lick the vulvas of females to evaluate their receptivity to breeding (sort of the canine equivalent of foreplay); females lick the penises of males to determine who they've been sleeping with, so to speak. Dogs lick one another out of affection, playfulness, deference ("Lick my boots, knave!"), and occasionally for the simple reason that there's something good to eat—a salty "eye booger," for example—clinging to the other dog's coat.

13.

WHY DO DOGS SNIFF THE BEHINDS OF OTHER DOGS?

The long and short of it is that this is how dogs identify and introduce themselves to one another, having found it extremely difficult—and not particularly enlightening—to shake hands and exchange the usual pleasantries. A dog sniffing another dog's "inguinal area," as the anatomical nether region is known, is essentially saying "Hello, who are you? Have we met before?"

Every dog has a unique scent "signature" created by the secretions of its anal sacs, a pair of small, kidney-shaped structures on either side of the anus. This signature not only serves to distinguish it from all other dogs, but apparently reveals whether the dog in question is male or female. And while scientists suspect that the scent signature relays additional information as well, they're still scratching their heads over exactly what that might be.

14.

WHY DO DOGS HAVE TO SMELL YOUR GUEST'S CROTCH?

This is a sort of corollary to #13. What you have to keep in mind is that to the average, well-socialized dog, humans are not different from them in kind, but only in degree—superior, albeit, from the dog's perspective, somewhat addled. Your dog considers you and your immediate family to be members of its pack, with each individual occupying a specific niche in the pack hierarchy. Typically, the dog assumes a subordinate role, although we're all familiar with households in which the dog rules the roost, as it were, having figured out that its people are either unable or unwilling to assert their dominance.

The upshot is that dogs sniff human crotches for the same reason they sniff canine rear ends: to establish identity. It's also likely that dogs are simply attracted by the bouquet of interesting aromas emanating from this region of the human body. A certain locational inevitability may be at work, too: All else equal, the muzzle of the average dog is carried at roughly the same level as the crotch of the average person.

15.

WHY DO ADULT DOGS CHEW ON BONES, RUGS, ANTIQUES, ETC.?

This is really a two-part question. All dogs, their age notwithstanding, chew on bones; that's simply a given. In evolutionary terms, bone-gnawing no doubt became instinctive because the wolves that indulged in it, even after every molecule of meat was gone, kept their teeth and gums healthier, longer, and thus gained an advantage in the struggle for survival. Rugs, antiques, and the like are a somewhat different matter (although there is a certain indiscriminateness at the heart of the chewing impulse).

Assuming your dog knows better—one of the proverbial "big ifs"—chewing these off-limits items probably reflects its feeling that it isn't receiving enough attention. To paraphrase the famous remark made by Glenn Close's chilling character in Fatal Attraction, the typical dog will not be ignored—especially a house dog that's accustomed to lots of praise, petting, and play. It's analogous to the child of inattentive or preoccupied parents who not only purposely commits some petty household crime but makes sure he gets caught. The way the kid—or the dog—sees it, it's better to risk a scolding than to remain invisible. Of course, there could also be a revenge factor involved, which would explain why your dog zeroes in unerringly on your most valuable piece of furniture.

16.

WHY DO DOGS INSIST ON SLEEPING IN BED WITH YOU?

What self-respecting dog would choose to sleep on the floor when there's a warm, soft, comfortable bed available? It would be like turning down champagne for club soda, or lobster thermidor for tuna surprise. Plus, in the context of the pack dynamic, the dog that's allowed to sleep with its alpha male and/or female feels as if it's climbed another rung on the social ladder. It's a kind of privileged access, like scoring a backstage pass to a Rolling Stones concert.

Of course, some dogs get a little greedy after they've had a taste of this pleasure, and begin to consider you the bed guest. You haven't really experienced sleeplessness until you've had to contort yourself around a dog that's claimed the center of the mattress and absolutely refuses to move. Dogs also snore, have convulsive dreams, and indulge in middle-of-the-night licking frenzies. In other words, letting your dog sleep with you is not necessarily a bed of roses.

17.

WHY DO KENNELED DOGS PACE ALL DAY?

They don't; they pace just long enough to lay a colossal guilt trip on you for not giving them more exercise, free play, field work, whatever. In dogs as in humans, pacing is a kind of pressure valve for the release of pent-up nervous energy, which explains why breeds that tend to be high-strung—field-bred pointers and English setters, for example—are also champion pacers.

It's likely, too, that it's an expression of the natural wanderlust common to the canid race, what Elizabeth Marshall Thomas, in her acclaimed *The Hidden Life of Dogs,* refers to as the desire for "voyaging." All creatures have daily (and seasonal) rhythms, and there are times when a dog simply needs to stretch its legs. Unable to hunt or voyage, the kenneled dog paces. The good news is that the confirmed pacer gives itself what amounts to a self-pedicure, meaning you don't have to clip its toenails very often.

18.

WHY DO RETRIEVING BREEDS RETRIEVE?

Virtually all dogs possess the retrieving instinct to some degree, the archetypal example being the dam who picks up a fugitive pup and "retrieves" it to the whelping pen. In the wild, of course, wolves retrieve small prey animals (or pieces of larger ones) for their young to feed upon. It's natural for dogs to pick things up in their mouths and carry them around—sticks, gloves, shed deer antlers, dead carp, etc.—and from there it's not a big step to get them to bring their booty to you . Praise and a tennis ball have probably taught more dogs to retrieve than any other method, ever.

What distinguishes the retrieving breeds—Labs, goldens, Chesapeakes, etc.—is their desire in this respect. If you want to get technical about it, this desire is a selective—i.e., human-induced—refinement of the basic prey drive; instead of taking the quarry (or its substitute) in its jaws and killing it, the retriever takes it in its jaws and tenderly (you hope) delivers it to hand. Dogs recognized as retrievers have existed since the 16th century (if not earlier); in the late-18th and early 19th centuries, the progenitor of the modern Lab was used on the high seas to retrieve fish that had become disentangled from the nets. By breeding one dog with a strong inclination to retrieve to another, the retrieving instinct was eventually "fixed," with the development of the specific breeds we know today not coming until later.

19.

WHY DO POINTING BREEDS POINT?

When a mammalian predator stalks its prey, it typically "freezes" for a few moments before springing into action. This hesitation is at the root of the pointing instinct. While various hound-type dogs had been employed for millennia to successfully hunt and capture four-footed game, birds were a different story. Dogs could find them, but finding them usually meant putting them to wing. And unless you were a nobleman with a falcon, a flushed bird was a lost bird in those pre-firearm days. But some insightful soul observed that a few dogs occasionally hesitated, momentarily transfixed, when they encountered scent. If the dog could be trained to "set" its birds rather than flush them, a hunter might be able to sneak up and cast a net over them.

Indeed, the earliest written accounts of pointing dogs, dating to the 13th century, would seem to indicate that it was more a trained behavior then than an instinctive one. By the 16th century, however, when "fowling pieces" were beginning to come into widespread use, selective breeding had produced dogs with a pronounced natural tendency to point. By that time, too, the two basic divisions of pointing dogs had been established, with the shorthaired breeds known generically as "pointers" and the longhairs as "setters" or "setting dogges." At its best, the point not only indicates the presence and location of game, but has the effect of making it "hold" until deliberately flushed by the hunter.

20.

WHY DO DOGS LIKE TO HANG THEIR HEADS OUT THE CAR WINDOW?

Let's clear the air right now and stress that, unless you're prepared to equip him with goggles, this really isn't a good thing to let your dog do. Neither is letting your dog ride loose in the back of the pickup, a practice that strikes me as the equivalent of riding a motorcycle without a helmet: It's fine—until it isn't.

Beyond the fact that the average image-conscious dog looks major cool with his ears flapping in the wind and a silly grin on his face (the envy of all his kenneled, fenced-in, and otherwise tethered brethren), I think the answer lies in those 220 million scent receptors stuffed inside his snout. A dog's sense of smell is its primary means of apprehending its world, a world that, given our own pitiful olfactory powers, we can scarcely imagine. And a dog shut up inside a car experiences the same kind of sensory deprivation you and I would if we were locked inside a darkened room. So when it sticks its head out the window, it's essentially flipping on the floodlights. Even when the window's barely rolled down, the typical dog will wedge his nose into the crack—just to see what is going on out there.

21.

WHY DO DOGS NAP SO OFTEN?

This question, I think, betrays a certain cultural bias. By American standards, yes, dogs take frequent naps. But in America sleeplessness—or, more precisely, the ability to *function* without sleep—is seen as a badge of honor. Instead of emulating the custom of more advanced nations and indulging in regular siestas, we gulp coffee, pop No-Doz, and generally do whatever it takes to stay awake when the civilized choice would be to recline, relax, and check our eyelids for leaks. It's almost as if we consider the nap somehow morally offensive, a reflection of deep, dark failings. There's also the vividly imagined fear that if we take a nap, the competition—whoever or whatever that might me—will get the drop on us.

Blissfully unencumbered by such baggage (or by the various other demons that plague the late-20th century American mind), the dog with nothing better to do and all its basic needs satisfied settles in for a snooze. Unlike us, dogs don't fight their nature. If it feels good, and the laws of the "pack" don't prohibit it, they do it. And, as Elizabeth Marshall Thomas observed, dogs relish the opportunity to simply "do nothing."

22.

WHY DO DOGS BEG FOR FOOD?

Setting aside the question of whether or not dogs should even *get* table scraps, it would be hard to cite a more clear-cut example of the power of positive reinforcement—which is to say, dogs beg for food because it's a tactic that works. The desired result—a morsel of the good stuff on *your* plate—is achieved. Over time, of course, each dog perfects its individual style in this regard, from the classic "sit up and beg" posture to the nudge-and-whimper, the sad, discomfiting stare, the muzzle-on-the-thigh, and various unbearably irresistible permutations thereof. An English setter of my acquaintance not only sits up and begs, but crosses his forepaws when he does so. Needless to say, his prowess as a panhandler is legendary.

Some dogs even learn that the best way to beg for food is to pretend not to, and that the probability of reward increases markedly by feigning complete indifference. Don't be fooled: These sharps know exactly what they're doing.

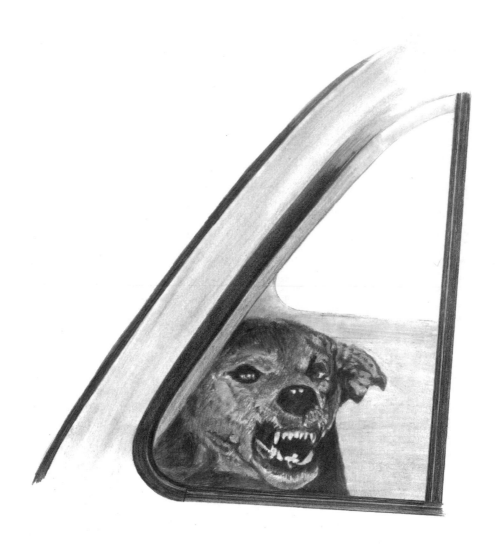

23.

WHY DO DOGS IN PARKED CARS TEND TO GROWL AND BARE THEIR TEETH?

One of the few hard-and-fast rules governing human-canine interaction is that you should never, ever, under any circumstances approach a strange dog that's shut in a car. (With the possible exception of a dog that's obviously in trouble because its moron owner shut it in on a hot day and didn't crack the windows.) This is why police vehicles assigned to "K-9" units have stern "Stay Back!" warnings printed on them.

Leaving a dog in a car brings out the most extreme form of its sense of territoriality. In the dog's mind, it's been charged with the duty of defending the property of the "pack," not to mention itself and its own "space." The dog is also put in the proverbial back-against-the-wall position, with nowhere to run and nowhere to hide should it be confronted by an aggressor it would normally flee from. The upshot is that it feels compelled to make a display of force at even the remotest suggestion of a threat—and it construes its threats very broadly. (Frankly, it's not a great idea to approach a strange dog in *any* situation without the consent and facilitation of its owner. In dogs as in people, looks can be deceiving.)

24.

WHY DO DOGS CHASE CATS?

Because it's so dang much fun, that's why. While it's inaccurate to claim, as so many "authorities" have, that dogs and cats are "natural enemies," there's no doubt that the average dog takes a special delight in running a cat up a tree. After all, the cat is the Anti-Dog: insolent, untrustworthy, conniving, mercenary in its loyalties, heinously and repugnantly *feline*.

What dog worth its salt wouldn't try to put such a fiendish, irredeemable beast to rout, especially one that spits, hisses, arches its back debauchedly, and utters weird, unearthly moans? In this respect, the cat-chasing dog is merely fulfilling the destiny for which its forebears were domesticated 15,000 years ago: to serve mankind. The alternative explanation is that (A) dogs chase things (as noted previously) and (B) cats are handy.

25.

WHY DO DOGS GULP THEIR FOOD RATHER THAN SAVOR IT?

To tell the truth, some dogs are dainty, finicky eaters—much to the consternation of their owners, who, in a role-reversing twist, often themselves assume the role of beggars, coaxing and cajoling their precious pet to take one more itsy-bitsy bite. In the main, however, it must be admitted that dogs display an appalling lack of table manners. They don't eat their food; they Hoover it, gobbling it up so fast and furiously that it's a wonder they don't black out for forgetting to breathe. (Whoever coined the term "chow hound" knew what they were talking about.)

But it isn't simply the *rate* of ingestion that's remarkable, it's the *volume*, too. Long before Beldar Conehead uttered the immortal words "Let us consume mass quantities," dogs were doing just that: They've been known to bolt as much as one-fifth of their body weight in food in a single belly-busting session. The explanation for this gluttonous behavior lies in the competition that occurs whenever "social carnivores"—i.e., wolves—bring down prey. If not exactly a case of winner-take-all and devil-take-the-hindmost, the animal that made quick work of feeding put itself in a better position to survive and pass along its genes. So when you accuse your dog of "wolfing down" its food, you're using precisely the right metaphor.

26.

WHY DO SOME DOGS HOWL?

"Some" is definitely the operative word here. Some dogs howl frequently, even incessantly; some dogs howl rarely, or only when prompted by the howling of others; some dogs never seem to howl at all. I could get my old English setter, Zack, to howl simply by blowing a few plaintive notes on a cheap harmonica, and my impression is that male dogs are more inclined to howl than females.

It also has been observed that "wolfish" breeds—huskies, for example—tend to be particularly enthusiastic howlers. Dogs—like wolves, and like their cousin the coyote, a.k.a. the "songdog"—howl for a bewildering variety of reasons: to communicate to other members of the pack, to signal their location, to proclaim the end of the day, to welcome the dawn, to greet the moon, and to express the entire gamut of emotions, from great joy to deep sorrow, enormous loneliness to profound contentment. Beyond a certain point, though, I don't think there's much to be gained by dissecting the root cause of howling. I mean, do a pub full of Irishmen need a reason to sing?

27.

WHY DO DOGS WALK IN A CIRCLE BEFORE LYING DOWN?

Robert Benchley, the acerbic humorist and unofficial chairman of the Adirondack Round Table, argued that one of the reasons a boy should have a dog is that "it teaches him to turn around three times before lying down." The "why" of this, however, has received surprisingly little attention from students of canine behavior. Folklore has it that dogs circle to flush out any snakes that might be lurking in the area. Given the fact that a snake-bitten dog of yore was unlikely to enjoy the opportunity to procreate, this explanation has a certain rough-hewn Darwinian logic.

A somewhat more plausible (albeit less colorful) theory, though, is that wolves circled in order to flatten the vegetation and simply make themselves more comfortable. Over the eons, this behavior became incorporated at the genetic level. The really interesting question (one that strikes me as the kind the late Ed Zern loved to ponder in his wonderful "Exit, Laughing" column in *Field & Stream*) is whether or not dogs in the northern and southern hemispheres, respectively, circle in different directions as a result of the Coriolis Effect.

28.

WHY DO WET DOGS ALWAYS SHAKE ON YOU?

This is one of those Law of Nature deals that defies logical explanation. The day you sell your stock is the day before a takeover bid doubles its price, when you discover a restaurant you really like it promptly goes belly-up . . . You get the picture. I suppose it could be argued that dogs shake on you because (A) they're not especially pleased at getting wet and they want you to know it, or (B) they're having so much fun in the water that they want to spread the happiness around. It could be, too, that they're so focused on the task at hand—retrieving a duck, for example—that they simply forget, and it doesn't even occur to them to shake until the job is finished. By then, of course, we're talking point-blank range.

29.

WHY DO DOGS EAT GRASS?

Remember, dogs are carnivores by nature, but omnivores by necessity. And by circumstance: When wolves bring down a moose, deer, caribou, or any of the other large herbivores that comprise the bulk of their diet, they immediately tear into its paunch, consuming not only the flesh and organs but vegetable matter in various states of digestion. The dog's desire for an occasional salad, therefore, is an atavistic expression of its racial memory, a harking back to the ways of its ancestors. And despite the "balanced nutrition" provided by most dog foods these days, there's something about a side of fresh greens (especially, it seems, in the springtime) that's awfully tempting. It could be the flavor, it could be the texture—no one really knows.

The problem is that the digestive system of the dog isn't well-equipped to handle the stuff "straight" (not partially pre-digested), which is why there's often a direct cause-and-effect relationship between grass-eating and upchucking. In fact, dogs suffering from an upset stomach will eat grass specifically to induce vomiting, hoping to purge whatever ill humors are affecting them.

30.

WHY DO DOGS PREFER OTHER DOGS' FOOD TO THEIR OWN — EVEN WHEN IT'S EXACTLY THE SAME?

Dogs are no different from kids in this respect. Children always seem to have a sneaking suspicion that they're getting the shaft, that their brother/sister/friend has a sweeter deal than they do. And even when you offer hard, objective proof to the contrary, they still believe, secretly, that the other kid not only has more of it—whatever "it" may be—but that it's bigger, better, and altogether cooler, too. This is why, if you place identical bowls of kibble in front of dogs occupying adjacent runs and leave the gates open, chances are they'll trade places in about two shakes of their tails. No doubt the dog's innate "food-competitiveness" (see also #25) plays a role in triggering this behavior as well.

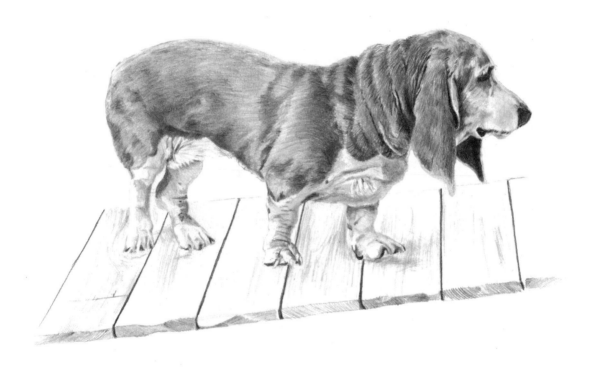

31.

WHY DO DOGS COME IN SO MANY SIZES, SHAPES, AND COLORS?

No species exhibits a greater degree of what scientists call "morphological variability" than the dog. It strains the imagination to look at a tiny, two-pound Chihuahua and a massive, 180-pound Saint Bernard and believe that they share the same basic genetic blueprint. Indeed, what's perhaps even more amazing than the dog's incredible range of physical variation is how little dogs vary at their most fundamental level. There are no genetic "markers," for example, that enable scientists to distinguish one breed from another. All appearances to the contrary, low-slung Dachshunds and towering Irish wolfhounds are more alike than different. The same goes for needle-nosed collies and scrunch-faced pugs, elegant Afghans and lumbering bulldogs, or any other pairing of opposites you can dream up from among the 400-plus breeds presently roaming the earth. (It's thought that as many as 1,000 distinct breeds have existed at one time or another.)

To account for the dog's diversity of sizes, shapes, colors, etc., you have only to consider that the species has been domesticated for 15,000 years—longer than any other animal—and that throughout this period humans have selectively bred it to display and embody characteristics they find useful, admirable, and attractive. It takes no great leap to grasp the enormity of the possibilities. The breeds we have today are their living proof.

32.

WHY DO DOGS RISK THEIR LIVES TO SAVE THEIR MASTERS?

The lore and literature of dogdom is replete with tales of canine courage, selflessness and sacrifice: the duck hunter whose boat capsizes in a snowstorm, only to be towed to shore by grasping the tail of the Labrador that swims in circles around him, refusing to leave his side; the child knocked out of the path of a speeding car by the mutt her parents rescued from the animal shelter; the family saved from asphyxiation by the cocker spaniel that wouldn't stop barking and scratching at the bedroom door until someone got up to investigate, then discovered the first insidious tendrils of smoke wisping up from the floorboards. Dogs have pulled people from the burning wreckage of cars and buildings and fought to repulse violent intruders even after suffering mortal wounds. Dogs have stayed with people who would have frozen to death without their warmth or summoned help when their masters suffered injuries far from civilization.

Little wonder that the dog, from the beginning of recorded history, has been considered the very exemplar of loyalty, embodying this quality to a degree we rarely find in ourselves. You could argue that the reason dogs perform these selfless acts is that they have no foreknowledge of death, and are thus unburdened by the free-floating fears and anxieties that so profoundly influence human behavior. Personally, I prefer to believe that dogs do such things because, despite their flaws, faults and idiosyncrasies, they are the finest and most inherently noble beings on the face of this earth.

33.

WHY DO DOGS PANT?

Dogs pant for some of the same reasons we do. For example, the anticipation of a pleasurable experience—for dogs, feeding time, going for a walk, being hitched to a sled—often leads to excited panting. Dogs also pant, obviously, in response to exertion. But the biggest reason dogs pant is that it's their primary means of dissipating heat and staying cool—in other words, regulating their body temperature. By rapidly moving air across the membranes in their mouths, moisture is evaporated. And as you recall from high-school physics, the process of evaporation draws off heat, thus cooling the affected surface. The same principle is at work when people sweat; it's just the mechanism that's different.

For the record, dogs do sweat—through the pads of their feet—but to such a negligible extent that canine physiologists dismiss the dog's sweat glands as "rudimentary" and "essentially non-functional." The problem with panting as a means of staying cool is that sometimes a dog simply can't keep up, particularly when high ambient temperature is coupled with high relative humidity. Once a dog's body temperature creeps above 104°F (the upper end of normal is 102°), heatstroke—or worse—becomes a distinct possibility. This is why no conscientious person ever confines a dog in a car during hot weather. It's a tragedy waiting to happen.

34.

WHY DO DOGS SEEM TO UNDERSTAND AND RESPOND TO OUR MOODS?

It's often said that dogs can "sense" our moods, and no one who's spent any amount of time in their company would dispute this. Dogs are great empathizers, able not only to tune in to our emotional wavelength, but to give us precisely what we need: a boisterous greeting, a soulful, knowing gaze, a reassuring thump of the tail. If more people had dogs, there would be far fewer of what are known generically as "mental health professionals." Indeed, the therapeutic value of canine companionship, especially for those who are elderly, disabled, or alone, is well-documented; simply put, people who have dogs tend to be happier than those who don't.

Some observers, at a loss to explain the extraordinary insights of which dogs are capable, have credited them with a kind of ESP—a "sixth sense," if you will. There's actually a germ of truth in this contention: Dogs, after all, can hear things we can't (hence the so-called "silent" whistle), and the world revealed to them by their noses is as brilliant, distinct, and variegated as our world of sight. Given the fact that emotional turmoil is often expressed physiologically, it's not a stretch to argue that dogs can, on occasion, literally smell our moods. Think of it this way: If people can "smell fear" (as the PIs in detective novels always seem to do), dogs certainly can. Dogs are also masters at reading body language and picking up on subtle inflections of voice, manner, and carriage. You could almost say that they know us better than we know ourselves.

35.

WHY DO DOGS LICK PEOPLE? ARE THEY KISSING US?

It's either that they are kissing you, or a cheap ploy to clean up the blueberry muffin crumbs clinging to your chin. Personally, I happen to think that it *is* a dog's way of kissing, at least insofar as kissing can be broadly defined as any oral display of affection. And because most of us react with delight— or at least all true dog lovers do—we reinforce the behavior. What I find interesting is the variety of styles, from the frenzied, slobbery, rapid-fire approach to the slow, solemn measured one.

Zack, my English setter previously mentioned, was not big on showing affection. But whenever I'd let him ride in the front seat of the truck, he'd sit facing me, gravely look me in the eye for a moment or two, and then, starting at my chin and ending at the tip of my nose, give me one tender, deliberate lick. Never two, always and only one. Then, feeling that he'd expressed as much emotion as the moment warranted, he'd curl up on the seat, using my thigh as a pillow for his unutterably lovely head. God, how I miss that dog.

36.

WHY DO DOGS LOVE TO CHEW SLIPPERS?

A little review seems to be in order here. We've established the fact that dogs like to chew; we've also established that they're peculiarly attracted to things of a somewhat "ripe" nature. Add these proclivities together, and it's easy to understand why a slipper, high with the Limburger smell of foot odor, is such a tempting target.

The average slipper also happens to fit quite comfortably into the mouth of the average dog. The texture and consistency are appealing, too, especially if the slipper's made of deerskin or a good, supple leather. Dogs enjoy chewing gloves for the same reasons; indeed, several highly regarded professional trainers use an old leather glove to encourage puppies to retrieve. Of course, it's impossible to mention dogs and slippers without recalling the classic, Rockwellian image of the man who, following a hard day at the office, returns home, settles into his easy chair, and bids his doting canine to fetch his pipe and slipper.

37.

WHY DO DOGS LOVE US EVEN AFTER PUNISHMENT, OR WHEN WE'VE LET THEM DOWN?

Because the love of a dog is almost wholly unconditional. There are no strings attached, no riders or special stipulations; there's no fine print, no expiration date, no statute of limitations. They love to a depth and degree that few of us, I fear, reciprocate, and if we're quick to forgive them, they're even quicker to forgive us. Their love is of an order that we probably don't deserve, and when we know that we have wronged them, acting out of anger or ignorance or sheer stupidity, their unwavering devotion shames us. There is nothing on this earth more heart-rending, more awful, than the pleading look in the eyes of a dog that cannot understand why the person it loves to the very marrow has caused it pain.

Why dogs should so single us out for favor, giving in vastly greater proportion to what they receive in return, is a question that really can't be answered. It defies all logical explanation—and yet it explains everything, too, because when you strip away the intervening layers, it is this fierce, abiding, unconditional love that ultimately defines Dog. It is also why the dog, of all the creatures that inhabit this chaotic ark, is the one most surely infused by the spark of the divine.

38.

WHY DO DOGS STEAL OUR HEARTS?

Does the phrase "beyond redemption" mean anything to you? Dogs steal our hearts because they touch us in ways that nothing else does, and in places that nothing else can reach. They move us with their courage, loyalty, and resolve; they astound us with their athletic prowess and the awesome capabilities of their noses; they delight us with their playfulness and eagerness-to-please; they comfort us with their uncanny ability to peer into our souls.

The bond between dogs and people has been forged by 15,000 years of mutual admiration and mutual trust. Civilizations have risen and fallen, the terrifying unknown has been explored, the great obstacles to human progress surmounted. And it has all been done with the dog—partner, companion, protector—at our side. Dogs don't steal our hearts; we surrendered our hearts to them long, long ago.

39.

WHY DO SLED DOGS PULL?

The Romans used a large, mastiff-type dog called a "molossus" as a draft animal; that is, an animal used to "draw" a load. And there's no doubt that dogs had been similarly employed for thousands of years by the time the Romans got around to writing about it. The breeds known collectively as "sled dogs"—the malamute, Samoyed, Siberian husky, etc.—are derived from the dogs used by indigenous Arctic tribes, although there is some debate in the anthropological camp as to when these peoples actually became mushers. Interestingly, the "Alaskan husky"—the dog that professional sled-dog racers, such as those who compete in the Iditarod, use almost exclusively—is not a recognized breed at all. Rather, it is a continuously evolving genre, a dog bred and developed not according to an arbitrary standard of appearance, but to a rigorous standard of performance. What is important is not the pedigree, but the contribution the individual dog can make in the way of increased speed, endurance, trainability, and/or leadership.

Unlike pointing or retrieving, behaviors that can be viewed as refinements to the dog's basic prey drive, pulling probably originated as something dogs were simply taught to do, something suited to their physical and mental constitutions. Over the millennia, as the dogs exhibiting the most ability in this regard were selectively bred, the sled dog "type" emerged. The fact of the matter, though, is that many dogs, regardless of breed, just seem to get a kick out of pulling.

40.

WHY DO GREYHOUNDS RACE?

Greyhounds belong to a class of dogs known as "sight hounds" or, more poetically, "gazehounds." By either name, it refers to a dog developed to run down visually targeted prey in open country (as opposed to "scent" hounds that rely almost entirely on their noses and rarely, if ever, sight their prey before it is brought to bay). The gazehound was, in all likelihood, the first dog bred for a specific purpose, and thus the first true breed. Dogs remarkably similar in appearance to the Saluki are depicted in 5,000-year-old Egyptian tomb paintings. The Saluki, of course, is essentially a greyhound with feathers (feathers in this sense being the long hair on the ears, tail, and legs). And, a smooth-coated dog fitting the greyhound profile to the proverbial T was described by the Roman poet, Ovid, at about the same time that a carpenter's son was beginning to stir things up in Galilee. It's probable, in fact, that the Romans originally brought the greyhound to England, where, over the centuries, the sport of "coursing" emerged as a means to determine who had the fastest dog.

In the 20th century, the mechanical "bunny" replaced the live hare, and greyhound racing as we know it was born. All of which is a roundabout way of explaining that greyhounds race because they have been bred for thousands of years to have a burning desire to chase things, and to be endowed with the blazing speed necessary to catch them.

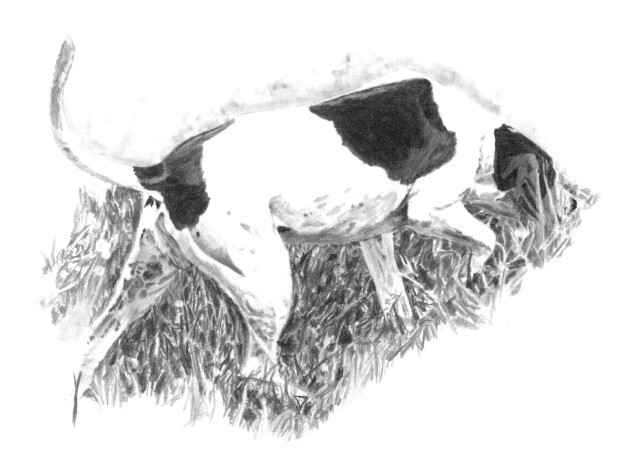

41.

WHY DO HOUNDS FOLLOW TRACKS?

There's no doubt that one of the earliest functions of the dog was to help human hunters locate, track, and recover game animals that were relied upon for food. It was simply a matter of harnessing and directing the dog's natural predatory instincts—letting it "follow its nose," so to speak. And that, essentially, is what hounds do. The development of bona fide "scent" hounds seems to have begun about 2,500 years ago in classical Greece, and was in full swing by the time the Romans first described the bloodhound in the third century AD. Medieval writers on sport list a bewildering variety of hounds—lymers, alaunts, etc.—each of which was prized for the unique talents it brought to the hunt of the stag or the boar, the principal quarry of antiquity. The word "quarry," in fact, derives from a French term for the ritual distribution of tidbits from slain prey to the dogs that participated in its capture.

In the lexicon of the houndsman, a "cold nose" refers not to the way a dog's nose feels against your skin, but to its ability to pick up a "cold"—as in not fresh—trail. This is an extremely important quality in bloodhounds, which are often used to find people lost in remote areas or to track down fugitives from justice. In hounds used for sport, however—coon hounds, foxhounds, beagles—a nose that's too cold can be a liability. There's a fine line between an exciting hunt and a wild goose chase, and a dog that "strikes" or "opens"—that is, gives tongue—on old scent tends to precipitate the latter.

42.

WHY ARE DOGS DISTRUSTFUL OF SOME STRANGERS AND NOT OTHERS?

While it's very politically correct to own a dog—and, from what I've read lately, a great way for single people to get dates—dogs themselves are very politically *incorrect*. They are unrepentant and irremediable stereotypers, drop-outs from Logic 101 who persist in falling into the trap of inductive reasoning. Which is to say, if a dog has a bad experience with a cigar-smoking man wearing sunglasses and a dark, three-piece suit, it's going to view every person who fits this description with deep suspicion. This is why, again, it's always a good idea, when you're meeting a dog for the first time, to have the owner facilitate the introduction. For all you know, the dog could have been mistreated by someone who used the same aftershave that you do, and, as the saying goes, once bitten, twice shy.

In the wild, obviously, where giving the benefit of the doubt tends to have a negative effect on one's longevity, this trait makes a lot of sense. There is very little survival value in regarding a lion, for example, as an individual rather than as a representative of a certain class. Again, this is an area in which some observers believe that dogs are able to "sense" the evil that lurks in the hearts of men. The more likely explanation is that a person with bad intentions telegraphs them in subtle ways that dogs, being keen observers, pick up on even when we don't. Unfortunately, dogs are not infallible in this respect, as many postal service employees are painfully aware.